C000142937

CONTENTS

2 **Getting Started**

4 **Reading Music**

SONGS

8 **CALL ME MAYBE** Carly Rae Jepsen

10 **HEY, SOUL SISTER** Train

12 **HO HEY** The Lumineers

14 **HOME** Phillip Phillips

16 **I KNEW YOU WERE TROUBLE.** Taylor Swift

18 **PARADISE** Coldplay

20 **SOME NIGHTS** fun.

22 **WHAT MAKES YOU BEAUTIFUL** One Direction

What fun is in store for you today! This RECORDER FUN!™ Songbook will have you playing the recorder quickly and easily while you learn to play your favorite songs.

ISBN 978-1-4803-6710-4

7777 W. BLUEMOUND RD. P.O. BOX 13819 MILWAUKEE, WI 53213

E-Z Play Today® Music Notation © 1975 by HAL LEONARD CORPORATION
E-Z PLAY and EASY ELECTRONIC KEYBOARD MUSIC are registered trademarks of HAL LEONARD CORPORATION.

Visit Hal Leonard Online at
www.halleonard.com

GETTING STARTED

HOLDING THE RECORDER

Here is how to hold the recorder. The mouthpiece rests on your lower lip, just like a drinking straw, with only a little of it actually going inside your mouth. Be sure that all of the finger holes line up on the front of the recorder as shown in the picture.

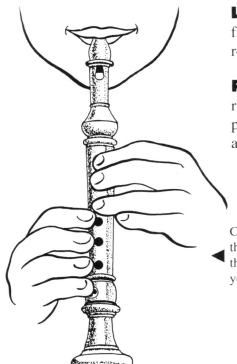

LEFT HAND — The first three fingers of your left hand (the little finger is not used) play the *top* three holes on the front of the recorder. The thumb of your left hand plays the hole on the back.

RIGHT HAND — The *bottom* four holes are played by your right-hand fingers. There is no hole for your right-hand thumb to play so it can help hold the recorder steady while the other fingers are busy playing.

◄ Cover the top three holes with your left-hand fingers and the bottom four holes with your right-hand fingers. The thumb of your left hand covers the hole in the back of your recorder.

MAKING A SOUND

To make a sound on the recorder blow gently into the small opening at the top of the mouthpiece. You can change this sound by covering different holes with your thumb and fingers. For example, when you cover all of the thumb and finger holes you will get a low, quiet sound. When only one or two holes are covered the sound will be higher and much louder.

Here are some tips for getting the best possible sound out of your recorder:

Always blow gently into the mouthpiece — Breathe in and then gently blow into the mouthpiece as if you were sighing or using a straw to blow out a candle. Remember, always blow gently.

Leaks cause squeaks — Play the holes using the pads of your fingers and thumb (not the tips). Press against each hole firmly so that it is completely covered and no air can sneak out. Even a tiny leak of air will change a beautiful tone into a sudden squeak!

Use your tongue to start each tone — Place your tongue against the roof of your mouth just behind your front teeth and start each tone that you play by tonguing the syllable "du" or "too" as you blow gently into the recorder.

PLAYING A TONE

Musical sounds are called *tones*. Every tone has a letter name. *Finger charts* are used to show you exactly which holes should be covered in order to play a particular tone. Each circle on these charts represents one of the holes on your recorder. The thumb hole is represented by the circle to the left of the recorder in the chart.

●   means that you should cover that hole.

○   means that that hole should not be covered but left open.

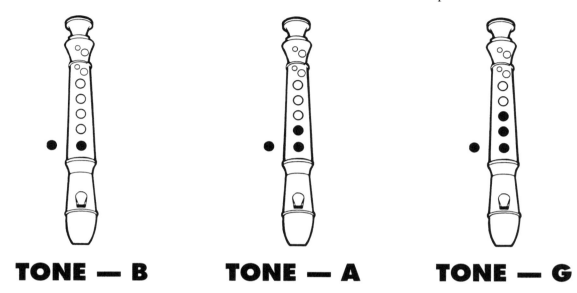

TONE — B   **TONE — A**   **TONE — G**

Use these three tones to play "Mary Had A Little Lamb:"

MARY HAD A LITTLE LAMB

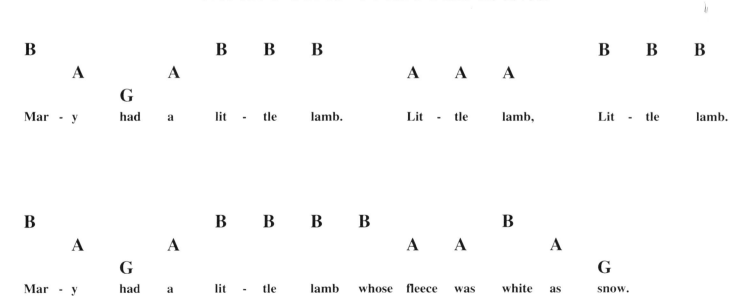

B				B	B	B					B	B	B
	A		A				A	A	A				
		G											
Mar - y	had	a	lit - tle	lamb.			Lit - tle	lamb,			Lit - tle	lamb.	

B				B	B	B	B			B			
	A		A					A	A		A		
		G										G	
Mar - y	had	a	lit - tle	lamb	whose	fleece	was	white	as	snow.			

READING MUSIC

Musical notes are an easy way to see everything that you need to know in order to play a song on your recorder:

How high or low — Notes are written on five lines that are called a *staff*. The higher a note is written on the staff the higher it will sound.

How long or short — The color of a note (black or white) tells you if it should be played short or long. The black notes in "Mary Had A Little Lamb" are all one beat long (*quarter notes*). The first three white notes in this song are two beats long (*half notes*) and the last note is four beats long (*whole note*).

How the beats are grouped — The two numbers at the beginning of the song (4/4) are called a *time signature*. This time signature tells you that the *beats* in this song are grouped in fours: **1** 2 3 4 **1** 2 3 4 etc. To help you see this grouping, *bar lines* are drawn across the staff to mark each *measure* of four beats. A *double bar* is used to mark the end of the song.

Now here is how "Mary Had A Little Lamb" looks when it is written in musical notes:

MARY HAD A LITTLE LAMB

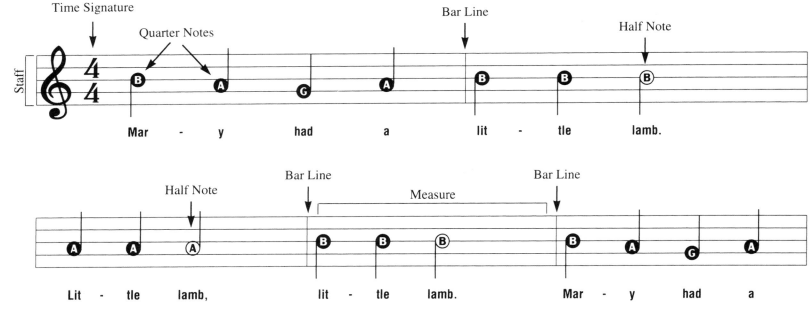

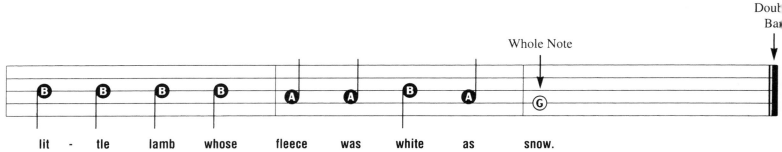

TWO NEW TONES

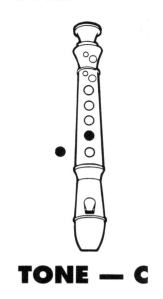

TONE — C

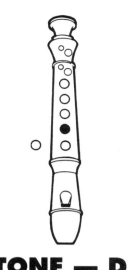

TONE — D

AURA LEE

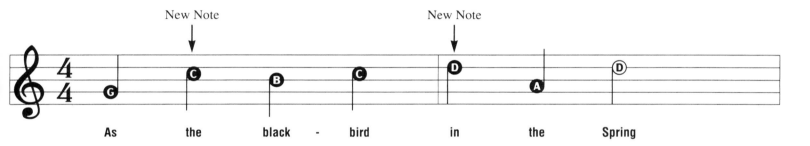

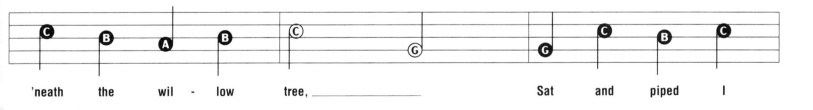

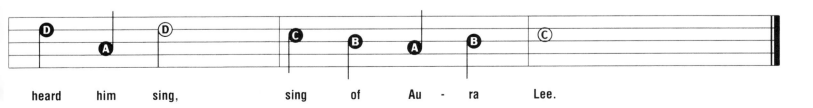

USING YOUR RIGHT HAND

"Twinkle, Twinkle Little Star" uses the tone E. As you can see from the fingering chart, you will use three fingers of your left hand and two fingers of your right to play this tone. The thumb hole is only half filled in (◑). This means that you should "pinch" the hole with your thumb so that only a small part of the hole is left open. Pinching is done by bending your thumb so that the thumbnail points directly into the recorder leaving the top of the thumb hole open.

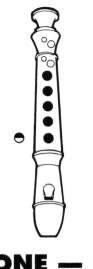

TONE — E

TWINKLE, TWINKLE LITTLE STAR

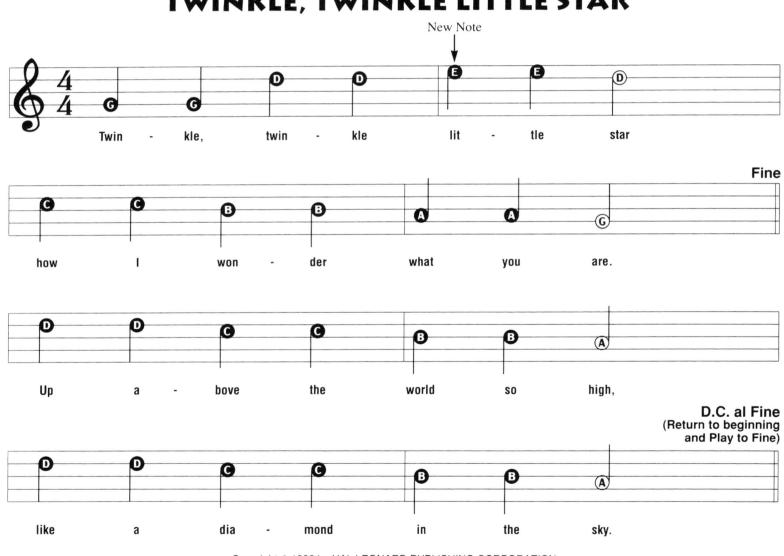

NOTES AND RESTS

In addition to notes that are one, two or four beats long, other values are possible. Also, *rests* are used to indicate when you should *not* play a tone but be silent. The chart on page 7 will help you identify the different notes and rests that are used in this book.

COUNT:

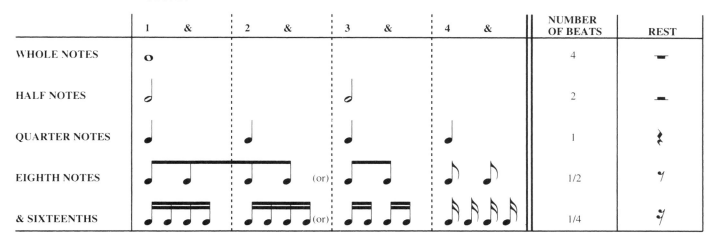

	1	&	2	&	3	&	4	&	NUMBER OF BEATS	REST
WHOLE NOTES									4	
HALF NOTES									2	
QUARTER NOTES									1	
EIGHTH NOTES			(or)						1/2	
& SIXTEENTHS			(or)						1/4	

DOTTED NOTES ARE 1 1/2 TIMES THE NORMAL LENGTH:

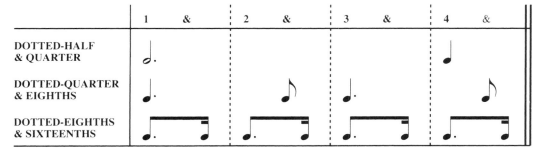

	1	&	2	&	3	&	4	&
DOTTED-HALF & QUARTER								
DOTTED-QUARTER & EIGHTHS								
DOTTED-EIGHTHS & SIXTEENTHS								

TRIPLETS ARE SPREAD EVENLY ACROSS THE BEATS:

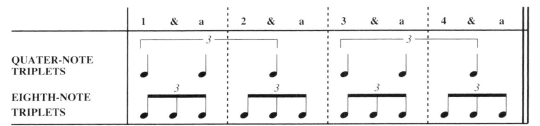

	1	&	a	2	&	a	3	&	a	4	&	a
QUATER-NOTE TRIPLETS												
EIGHTH-NOTE TRIPLETS												

THIS OLD MAN

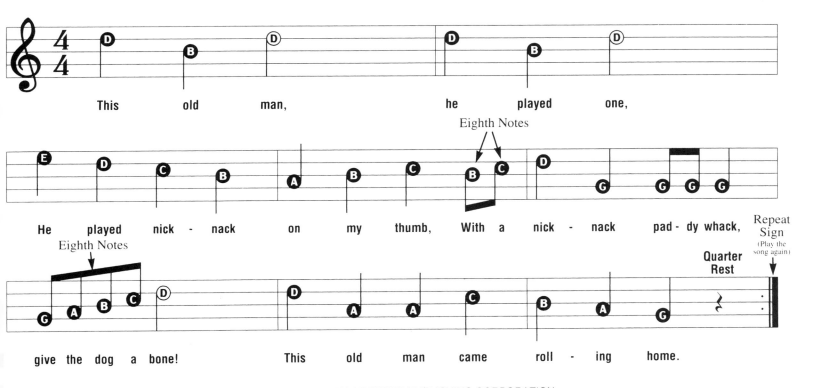

CALL ME MAYBE

Words and Music by Carly Rae Jepsen,
Joshua Ramsay and Tavish Crowe

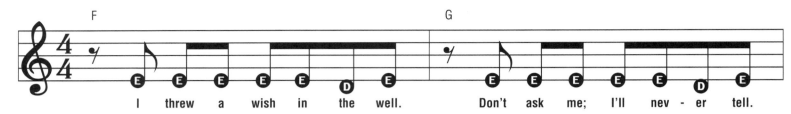

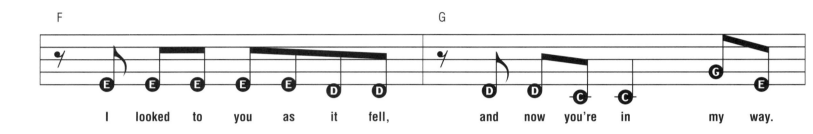

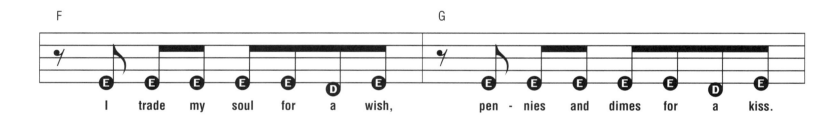

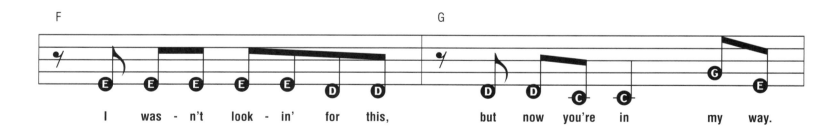

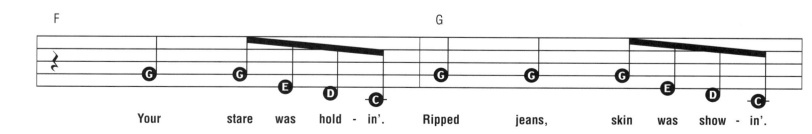

HEY, SOUL SISTER

Words and Music by Pat Monahan,
Espen Lind and Amund Bjorkland

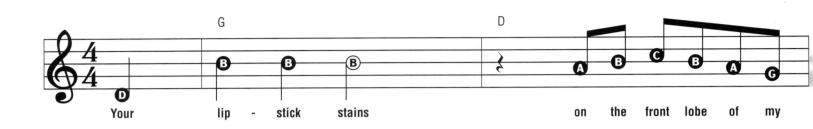

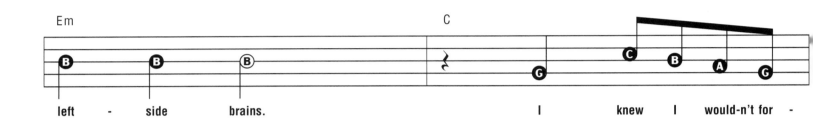

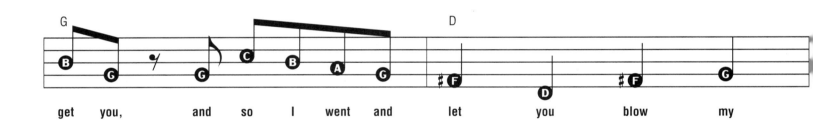

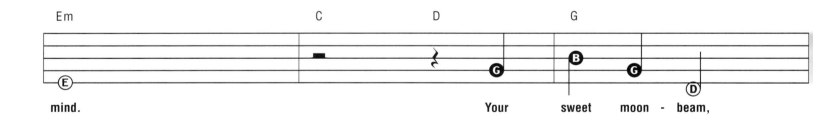

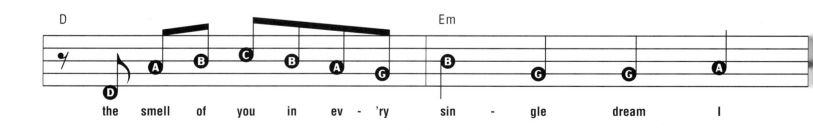

HO HEY

Words and Music by Jeremy Fraites
and Wesley Schultz

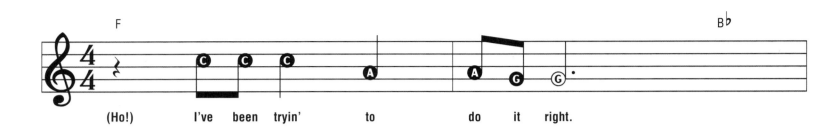

(Ho!)   I've been tryin'   to   do it right.

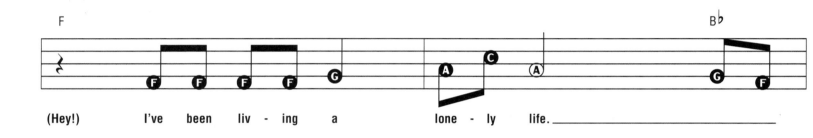

(Hey!)   I've been liv - ing a   lone - ly life. _____

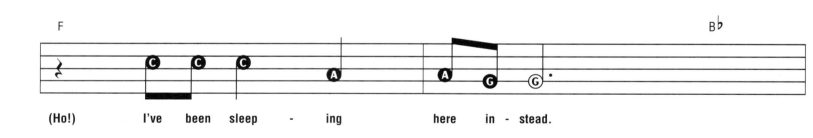

(Ho!)   I've been sleep - ing   here in - stead.

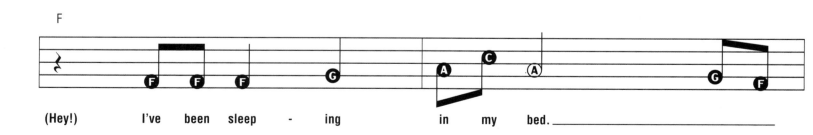

(Hey!)   I've been sleep - ing   in my bed. _____

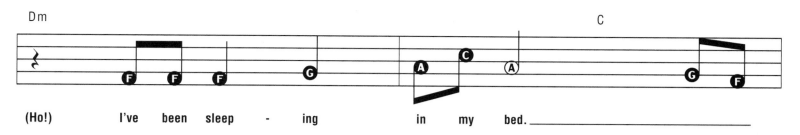

(Ho!)   I've   been   sleep - ing   in   my   bed._____

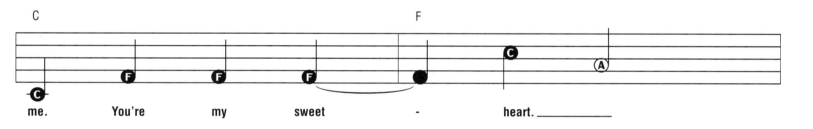

(Hey!)   I   be - long   with   you,   you   be - long   with

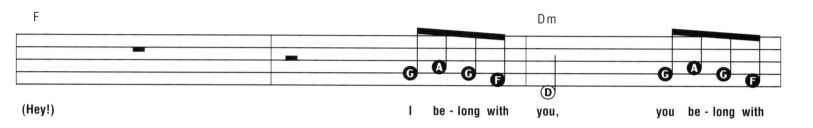

me.   You're   my   sweet -   heart._____

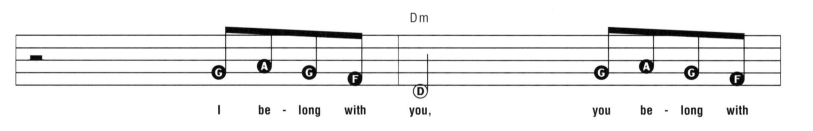

I   be - long   with   you,   you   be - long   with

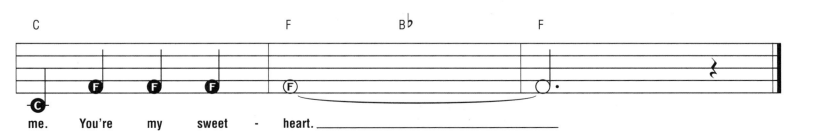

me.   You're   my   sweet -   heart._____

HOME

Words and Music by Greg Holden
and Drew Pearson

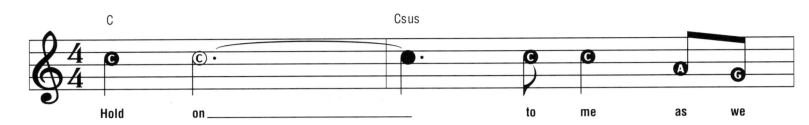

Hold   on _____   to   me   as   we

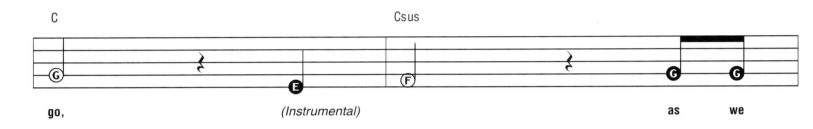

go,   *(Instrumental)*   as   we

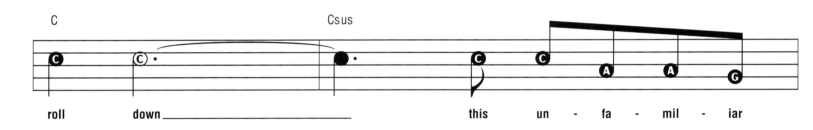

roll   down _____   this   un - fa - mil - iar

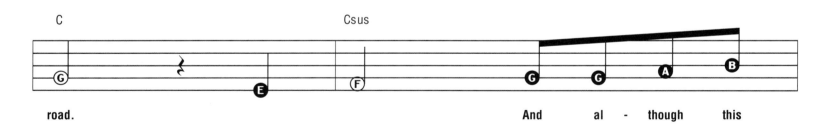

road.   And   al - though   this

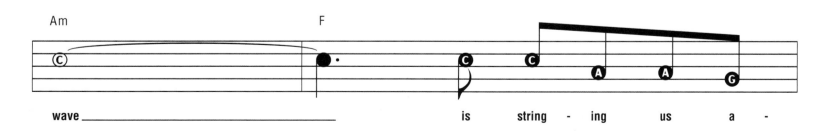

wave _____   is   string - ing   us   a -

long, just know you're not a - lone, 'cause I'm gon - na make this place your home. *(Instrumental)* Ooh, _____ ooh. _____ Ooh. _____

I KNEW YOU WERE TROUBLE.

Words and Music by Taylor Swift,
Shellback and Max Martin

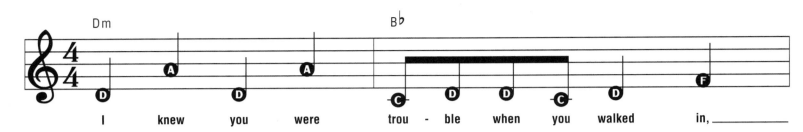

I knew you were trou - ble when you walked in, ____

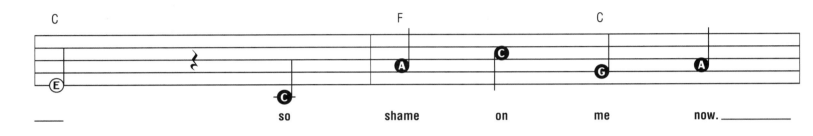

____ so shame on me now. ____

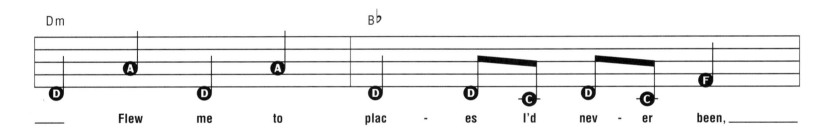

____ Flew me to plac - es I'd nev - er been, ____

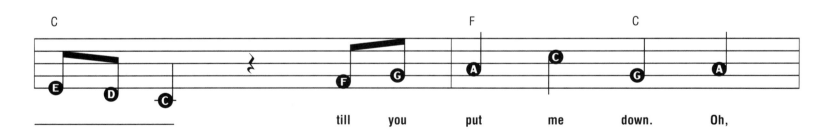

____ till you put me down. Oh,

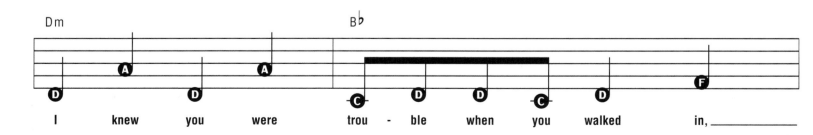

I knew you were trou - ble when you walked in, ____

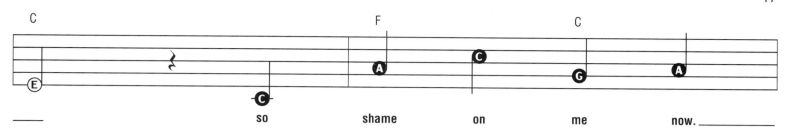

____ so shame on me now. _____

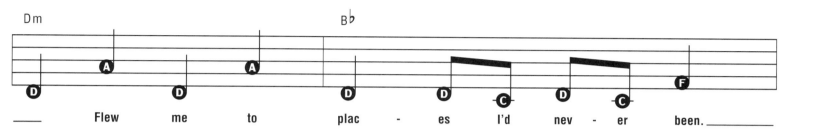

____ Flew me to plac - es I'd nev - er been. _____

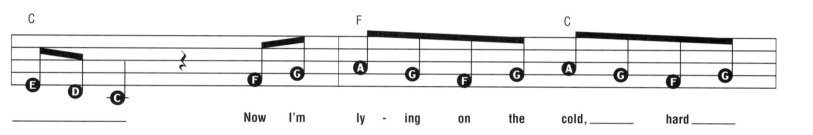

_____ Now I'm ly - ing on the cold, _____ hard _____

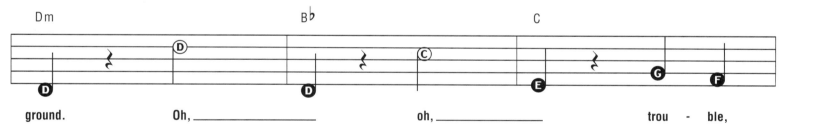

ground. Oh, _____ oh, _____ trou - ble,

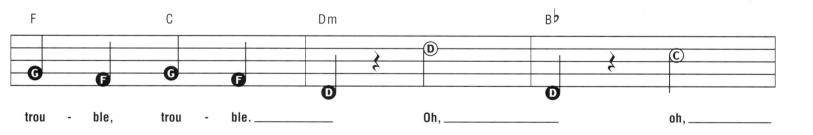

trou - ble, trou - ble. _____ Oh, _____ oh, _____

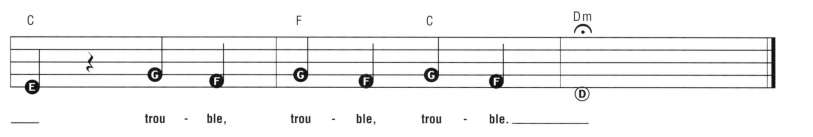

____ trou - ble, trou - ble, trou - ble. _____

PARADISE

Words and Music by Guy Berryman,
Jon Buckland, Will Champion,
Chris Martin and Brian Eno

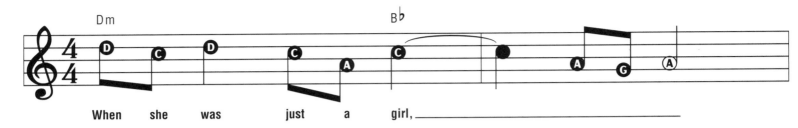

When she was just a girl,

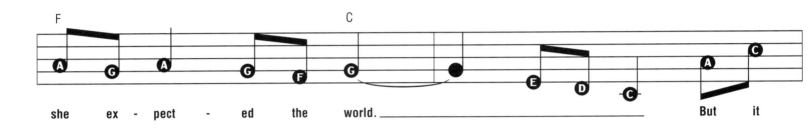

she ex - pect - ed the world. But it

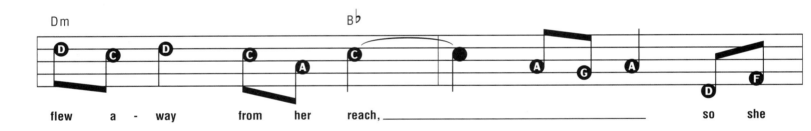

flew a - way from her reach, so she

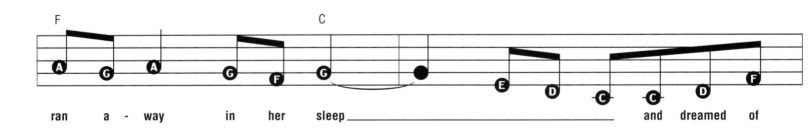

ran a - way in her sleep and dreamed of

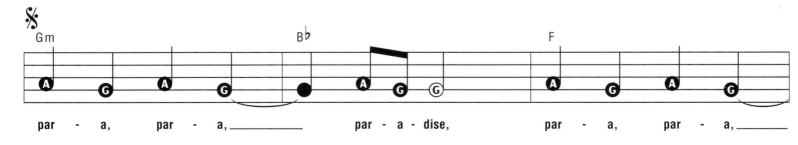

par - a, par - a, par - a - dise, par - a, par - a,

SOME NIGHTS

Words and Music by Jeff Bhasker,
Andrew Dost, Jack Antonoff
and Nate Ruess

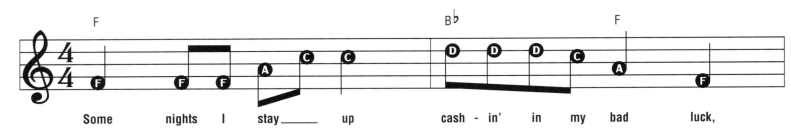

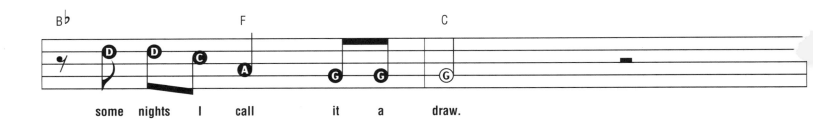

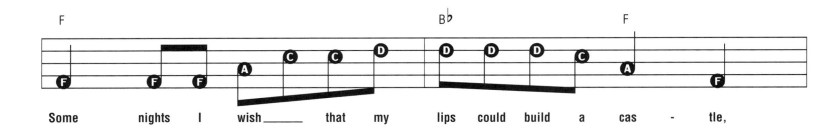

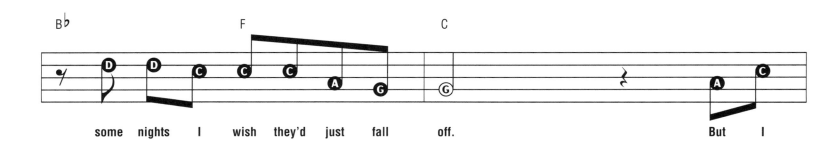

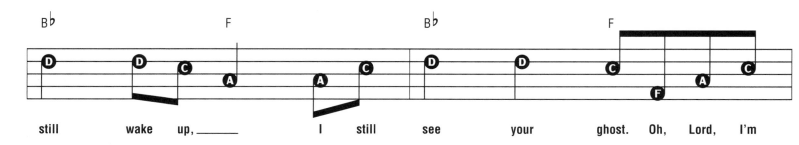

WHAT MAKES YOU BEAUTIFUL

Words and Music by Savan Kotecha,
Rami Yacoub and Carl Falk

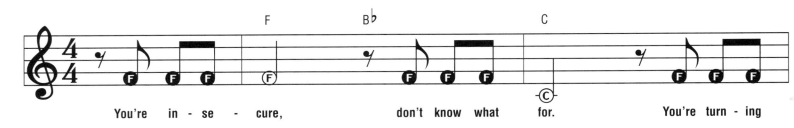

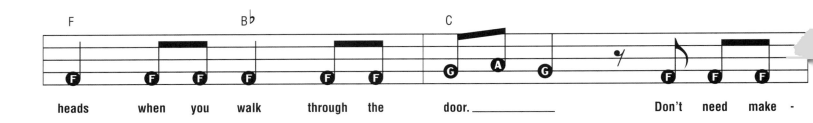

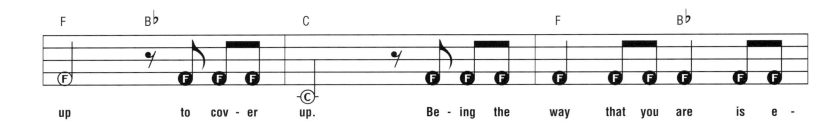

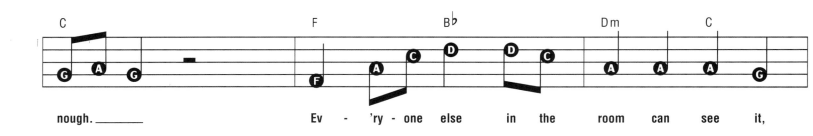

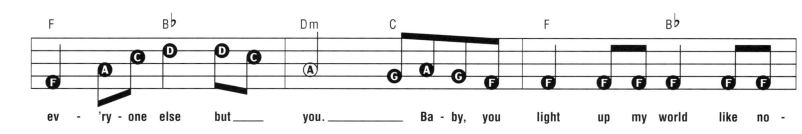

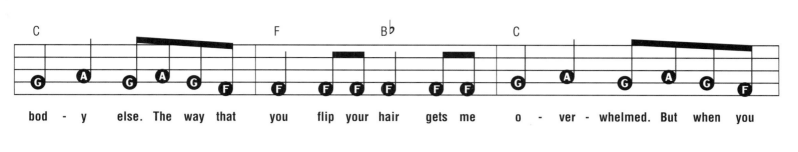

bod - y else. The way that you flip your hair gets me o - ver - whelmed. But when you

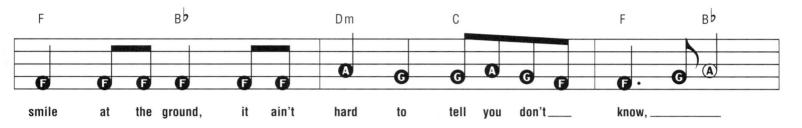

smile at the ground, it ain't hard to tell you don't___ know, _____

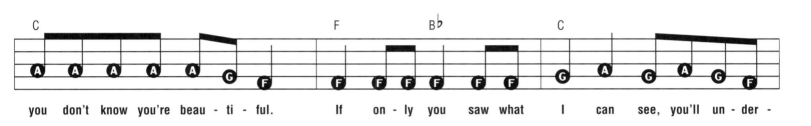

you don't know you're beau - ti - ful. If on - ly you saw what I can see, you'll un - der -

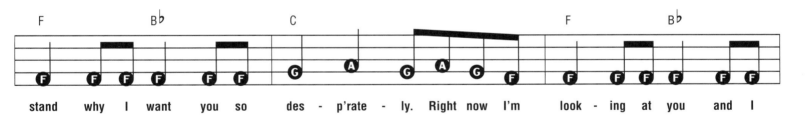

stand why I want you so des - p'rate - ly. Right now I'm look - ing at you and I

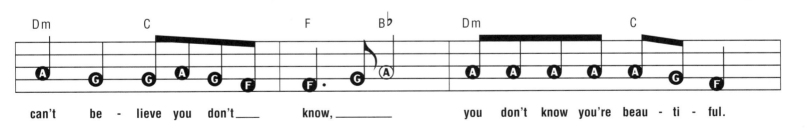

can't be - lieve you don't___ know, _____ you don't know you're beau - ti - ful.

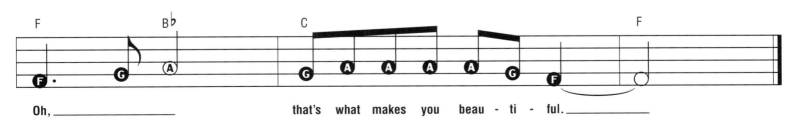

Oh, _____ that's what makes you beau - ti - ful._____

Your Favorite Songs Arranged for Recorder

THE BEATLES

Recorder arrangements for 18 Fab Four hits, including: All My Loving • Come Together • Day Tripper • Eight Days a Week • Hey Jude • In My Life • Let It Be • Michelle • Norwegian Wood • Penny Lane • With a Little Help from My Friends • Yesterday • and more. Includes a fingering chart.

00710152 .... $7.99

BEATLES HITS

15 Fab Four faves arranged for recorder: Blackbird • Eleanor Rigby • A Hard Day's Night • I Want to Hold Your Hand • The Long and Winding Road • Love Me Do • Nowhere Man • She Loves You • Ticket to Ride • When I'm Sixty-Four • Yellow Submarine • and more!

00710151 .... $7.99

BROADWAY FAVORITES

13 favorite showtunes arranged for recorder: Any Dream Will Do • As Long as He Needs Me • Consider Yourself • Getting to Know You • I Dreamed a Dream • Make Someone Happy • Memory • On a Clear Day (You Can See Forever) • On My Own • People • Sunrise, Sunset • Tomorrow • We Built This City.

00710141 .... $7.99

DISNEY HITS

15 beloved Disney hits arranged for the recorder, complete with a fingering chart! Songs: The Bare Necessities • Colors of the Wind • A Dream Is a Wish Your Heart Makes • Part of Your World • Reflection • Someday • A Spoonful of Sugar • When She Loved Me • Whistle While You Work • You'll Be in My Heart • You've Got a Friend in Me • Zip-A-Dee-Doo-Dah • and more!

00710052 .... $7.99

DISNEY MOVIE FAVORITES

Nine Disney classics arranged for recorder solo or duet: Be Our Guest • Beauty and the Beast • Can You Feel the Love Tonight • Circle of Life • Friend like Me • I Just Can't Wait to Be King • Kiss the Girl • Under the Sea • A Whole New World. Includes a helpful fingering chart.

00710409 .... $7.99

WALT DISNEY FAVORITES

Newly revised, this collection features 13 Disney hits arranged for recorder solo or duet, plus a handy fingering chart! Songs: The Aristocats • Candle on the Water • Chim Chim Cher-ee • Heigh-Ho • It's a Small World • Mickey Mouse March • Once upon a Dream • The Siamese Cat Song • Some Day My Prince Will Come • Supercalifragilisticexpialidocious • When You Wish upon a Star • Who's Afraid of the Big Bad Wolf? • Winnie the Pooh.

00710100 .... $7.99

FAVORITE MOVIE THEMES – 2ND EDITION

14 film favorites for recorder: Chariots of Fire • Dancing Queen • Forrest Gump – Main Title • He's a Pirate • I'm a Believer • It Will Rain • Mission: Impossible Theme • My Heart Will Go On • Tears in Heaven • and more.

00841306 .... $7.99

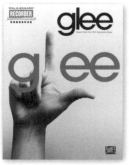

GLEE

Blow your heart out with this collection of 13 Glee standouts, arranged for the recorder – complete with a helpful fingering chart! Contains: Alone • Bad Romance • Defying Gravity • Don't Stop Believin' • Dream On • Hello • Lean on Me • Like a Prayer • No Air • Proud Mary • Rehab • The Safety Dance • Sweet Caroline.

00710056 .... $7.99

KIDS' SONGS

Features 13 songs kids adore, arranged for the recorder: The Addams Family Theme • Alley Cat Song • The Candy Man • Everything Is Beautiful • The Hokey Pokey • I Whistle a Happy Tune • Peter Cottontail • Puff the Magic Dragon • Sesame Street Theme • Sing • Take Me Out to the Ball Game • This Land Is Your Land • Won't You Be My Neighbor?. Includes a helpful fingering chart.

00710051 .... $7.99

THE SOUND OF MUSIC

Williamson Music

Features 13 tunes from the beloved Rodgers & Hammerstein classic arranged especially for recorder: Climb Ev'ry Mountain • Do-Re-Mi • Edelweiss • I Have Confidence • Maria • My Favorite Things • Sixteen Going on Seventeen • So Long, Farewell • Something Good • The Sound of Music • and more. Includes a fingering chart.

00710200 .... $7.99

STAR WARS

Features 15 iconic themes from all the *Star Wars* movies arranged for recorder! Includes: The Arena • Cantina Band • The Imperial March (Darth Vader's Theme) • May the Force Be with You • Parade of the Ewoks • Princess Leia's Theme • Star Wars (Main Theme) • Victory Celebration • Yoda's Theme • and more. Students will love playing these familiar themes while advancing through their recorder lessons!

00110292 .... $7.99

TAYLOR SWIFT

15 Swift hits arranged for recorder, including: Back to December • Eyes Open • Love Story • Mean • Should've Said No • Speak Now • Teardrops on My Guitar • Today Was a Fairytale • White Horse • You Belong with Me • and more!

00110275 .... $8.99

HAL•LEONARD CORPORATION

7777 W. BLUEMOUND RD. P.O. BOX 13819 MILWAUKEE, WI 53213

www.halleonard.com

1113